CARING FOR
• YOUR PET •

KITTENS AND CATS

Amanda Jane Sands

SMITHMARK

This edition published in 1996 by SMITHMARK Publishers, a division of U.S. Media Holdings, Inc., 16 East 32nd Street,New York, NY 10016.

1 2 3 4 5 6 7 8 9

SMITHMARK books are available for bulk purchase for sales promotion and premium use. For details write or call the manager of special sales, SMITHMARK Publishers 16 East 32nd Street, New York, NY 10016; (212) 532-6600.

ISBN 0 8317 6844 4

CREDITS
Editor: Marion Elliot **Design by:** DW Design, London
Color Separation by: Pixel Tech, Singapore
Filmset by: SX Composing Ltd., Essex
Printed in Slovenia

PICTURE CREDITS
Artists
Copyright of the artwork illustrations on the pages following the artist's name is property of Salamander Books Ltd.

Wayne Ford: 13, 15, 26, 56
Photographs
The publishers wish to thank the following photographers and agencies who have supplied photographs for this book. The photographs are copyright of the photographer and have been credited by page number and position on the page: (B) bottom, (T) top, (C) centre etc.

Marc Henrie: 8, 9, 10, 11, 15, 18, 32, 36, 46
Cyril Laubscher: 20, 21, 22, 27, 28, 31(B), 34, 37, 40
RSPCA Photolibrary: Judyth Platt; title; Steve Cobb; 7;
Dorothy Burrows, 12; Stuart Harrop, 13, 19, 61; Valerie Bissland, 17;
Ken McKay, 48; Julie Meech, 59; E.A. Janes, 63;
David Sands: 4, 6, 24, 25, 31(T), 38
Interpet Ltd: Bernard Bleach, 33
Jacket photograph © RSPCA, supplied by RSPCA Photolibrary

Contents

Introduction

Cats make delightful pets. They are more
independent than dogs and some breeds are suitable
for families that may be out at school and work
during the day. There is a large number of varieties
and breeds. The most widely available kinds are
non-pedigree short-haired cats that range from black
to tabby. There are many pedigree breeds too,
including Shorthair, Burmese, Siamese, and
long-haired Persians. The
short-haired varieties are easy
to groom compared
with the

long-haired varieties which require much more attention and will take up a lot of your time. Cats are sociable, friendly creatures and, with the correct care and attention, your kitten will grow up to be a happy cat with an affectionate personality.

Where cats come from

Miacids is the name given to early carnivores. It is thought that all cats including lions, tigers, and the pet cat, *Felis catus*, are descended from these animals. Some of the early carnivores developed into the larger felines, such as lions, tigers, and leopards. Other Miacids are thought to have evolved into smaller species of wild cats, like the African wild cat and the European wild cat.

Modern wild cats

Many wild cats are quite shy and usually live alone. The domestic cat is thought to be descended mainly from these animals and there are many similarities in size and color pattern. The tabby and spotted markings, which can be seen in our pet cats today are very similar to the markings of the wild cats. These coat patterns offer the wild cat excellent camouflage. Behavior traits and habits which are often seen in the domestic cats are also present in wild cats.

● *Left: A cheetah baring its teeth. All cats are thought to be descended from the same animals, the Miacids.*

Domesticated cats

Working cats

Cats were first tamed by the ancient Egyptians over 3,000 years ago. The Egyptians considered cats to be sacred and held them in high esteem. The cat, with its expert hunting techniques, became useful to the Egyptians and other civilizations as a means of keeping rats and mice from eating stores of grain. Their usefulness kept cats popular until the Middle Ages in Europe. However, about this time it was thought that cats were involved with witches and so they fell out of favor for a long time.

● **Above:** *Cats are great hunters. Here a feral cat (a domesticated cat that lives wild) has captured a shrew. In the past, cats were often used to guard grain stores because they were so good at catching rats and mice.*

Pet cats

By the eighteenth century, cats were popular again and they are now a favorite family pet. They make great companions and a well-cared-for cat can be a very special member of your household.

Feral cats

Groups of cats can sometimes be seen living on wasteland, especially around docks and empty buildings. These are known as feral cats. Feral cats are domesticated cats which are untamed and live wild. They differ from true wild cats because they often live in large colonies rather than on their own.

● *Above: Cats weren't always the popular pets that they are today. At one time, people associated cats with witches and so they were not made welcome. Nowadays, however, the cat ranks with the dog as one of the best-loved pets.*

7

Choosing the right breed

The new arrival
The arrival of a new cat or kitten will affect every member of your household, including other pets. You must make sure that everyone wants a cat before you decide to get one. Pick the breed which seems to fit in best with your lifestyle. For example, don't choose a cat that needs lots of company if you and your family are out of the house all day.

Popular breeds
There are many breeds and colors of cat. Coat markings vary from self (one solid color), to tabby (striped), to spotted. There are several basic body shapes to choose from, ranging from stocky and muscular to slim and sleek. Cats are also divided into short-haired and long-haired varieties.

Short-haired breeds
British Shorthair
These cats are large and muscular and come in a wide range of colors and coat patterns. Shorthairs are placid and friendly by nature and make ideal pets for owners who are not at home during the day.

Burmese

Burmese are medium-sized cats with sleek, short fur. They are intelligent, affectionate, and playful cats but they do not like to be left on their own all day.

● **Above:** Burmese cats have sleek fur.

Exotic Shorthair

These cats are the result of crossing long-haired with Shorthair cats. They have soft, thick coats in various colors. Exotic Shorthair cats are affectionate and playful.

● **Left:** An Exotic Shorthair cat has a soft, thick coat.

Siamese
Siamese cats are medium-sized and have slim, elegant bodies. They are intelligent, vocal, and affectionate. They dislike being left on their own all day.

Long-haired breeds

Birman
Birmans are medium-sized with stocky bodies. They are very friendly.

● *Above: The Siamese cat makes a very loyal pet and the Birman mixes well with other pets. (Below)*

Maine Coon
These cats are large

with muscular bodies. They have large ears. Maine Coons are playful, good tempered cats.

● *Left:* The Maine Coon is large and stocky.

● *Below:* Persians are sweet and gentle cats.

Persian

Persians are fairly large with sturdy bodies. They come in many colors. Persians are sweet and gentle and like being with people. They must be groomed every day as they molt heavily, so make sure that you will have enough time for grooming before you get a Persian cat.

Ragdoll

Ragdolls are large and muscular and come in several colors. They are quiet, playful and affectionate cats and make ideal family pets. They can grow noticeably larger than other breeds of cat and have very thick fur.

Picking a healthy pet
The healthy kitten's coat should be smooth and clean. Its eyes and ears should be clean. The gums should be pink and the teeth clean and unbroken. The nose should be clean and damp. If there are several kittens to choose from, pick one that is lively and playful. Don't choose a kitten which is timid or hiding in a corner just because you feel sorry for it. Kittens should be at least 10 weeks old and fully weaned before being parted from their mothers.

Pedigree cats
Pedigree cats are bred to a special standard and can be very expensive. There are three types, Show, Breeding and Pet. Show-quality cats are close enough to the special standard to compete in competitions. Breeding-quality cats will produce kittens that match the standard. Breeding cats is hard work and can be very expensive. Pet-quality cats aren't close enough to the standard to compete successfully in shows or breed, but they make good pets. Although pedigree kittens are expensive, the breeder will have a good idea of the cat's personality and adult appearance. Always feel free to ask your local vet to recommend a good cat breeder.

Non pedigree cats
Non pedigree cats are much cheaper than pedigrees and some are even "free to good homes." There are many abandoned kittens and cats needing loving homes. Details on charities that rescue cats can be obtained from your vet or the telephone book.

● *Above: There are many abandoned cats in shelters needing loving homes.*

A cat or a kitten?

Kittens need lots of attention. They require four or five meals a day and will become lonely if they are left on their own. They often need house breaking. All kittens need vaccinations and, unless they are to be kept for breeding, will need to be neutered between six and twelve months of age. Older cats only need feeding

● **Above:** *Kittens can be demanding. They need lots of attention in the early days.*

twice a day and are usually house broken. Providing that their new home is warm and friendly, mature cats take very little time to settle down.

Male or female?

All cats can make lovely pets. However if you don't have your pet neutered its behavior can be quite antisocial. Males will mark their territory by spraying strong-smelling urine inside and outside the house. Female cats will regularly come into season, which means that they are ready to mate. When this happens they become restless and yowl very loudly.

● **Left:** *It can be difficult to tell the sex of a kitten. Here, a female kitten is shown on the far left and a male kitten is on her right.*

13

Questions *and* Answers

Should I choose a kitten or an adult cat?
Kittens demand lots of attention and they need to be house broken. When young, they require small meals up to five times a day. Adult cats need less frequent meals and are usually already house broken. They can be "rescued" from animal charity shelters and given a good home.

Should I choose a pedigree or non pedigree kitten or cat?
Pedigree kittens and cats can be very expensive. They may not be as traffic-aware as other cats and are best kept indoors or allowed out in safe, specially made runs. Non pedigree kittens or cats are much cheaper and are sometimes even "free to a good home."

Should I choose a male or female?
Once your kitten or cat has been neutered there is little difference between the sexes. Male cats can be just as affectionate and homeloving as female cats.

Which is the best cat breed for me?
This depends on what you would like from your cat. For example, Shorthairs are generally quiet, calm, and quite independent, while Siamese cats require a lot of attention and don't like to be left on their own all day.

Are some breeds more talkative than others?
Most cats have a range of meows. Oriental breeds, such as the Siamese seem to "talk" more than most cats and are famous for their voices!

14

● **Above:** Kittens need a lot more attention than adult cats and will get lonely if they are left on their own.

15

Understanding your cat

The cat's skeleton
The cat's backbone is very flexible. The spine contains many loosely connected bones. Its flexible spine allows the cat to arch its back.

The tail
The cat's tail contains many small bones. It helps the cat to balance and change direction. A cat also uses its tail as a visual signal to express how it is feeling.

Defense
The claws are attached to the cat's toe bones. Tendons attached to the claws enable a cat to extend its claws forward and downward. A cat uses its claws to defend itself, mark its territory, or cling to surfaces when it is climbing.

KITTEN • CAT • CARE

The fur

The cat's fur helps to keep its body dry and at the correct temperature. Domesticated cats molt all year round. Wild cats molt only in winter when a new, extra warm coat is needed.

Grooming the fur

Cats will spend a lot of time grooming. During grooming, the cat licks its fur with its tongue, which is covered with small bumps. Cats also use their front paws to brush and smooth their fur.

● *Above and left: Cats have very flexible backbones and sharp claws.*

● *Right: Cats are very clean and groom their fur with their tongues and their front paws.*

Designed for hunting

A cat has 30 teeth. Most of the teeth are sharp and enable the cat to kill and eat its prey. The fangs (canine teeth) are very large and help a cat to bite into the neck of its prey. The back teeth (molars) are used to cut meat up into small pieces.

Hearing

A cat's hearing is very sensitive. This enables it to wait and hide itself so it can pounce on its prey.

● *Above: A hunting cat hides in the undergrowth and watches quietly. Cats have a highly-developed sense of hearing, which they use when they are stalking their prey.*

● *Above:* Cats are able to see in poor light conditions because the backs of their eyes reflect back light.

Sight

Kittens are blind for about the first seven days. Their vision gradually improves until, at twelve weeks, their sight is fully developed. Cats can see well in semidarkness or poor light because the backs of their eyes act like mirrors and reflect back light.

Getting around

Whiskers allow the cat to "feel" and measure its way around. It is said that if the width of a cat's whiskers fit through an opening, it knows that its whole body will also be able to pass through the same space.

Making your cat comfortable

Beds

Cats love to be comfortable and there are lots of different cat beds available. The range includes wicker baskets, bean bags, and even hammocks that can be hung on radiators. The bed should be warm and easy to clean. Position the bed in a quiet, draft-free place in your home so that your pet can have some privacy.

● *Above:* A comfortable wicker basket with rounded sides to keep out drafts makes the perfect bed for your cat.

Scratching post

Cats and kittens need to scratch to keep their claws in good condition. If your pet hasn't got a scratching post it will probably use your furniture instead. You can buy several kinds from a pet supply store, including ones which smell of cat mint to encourage cats to use them. You could also give your cat a wooden log to use. It will enjoy scratching against the texture of the bark.

● *Above:* Cats keep their claws in good condition because they use them for defense. They will constantly scratch against objects to sharpen their claws. To prevent your pet from damaging furniture you should provide it with a scratching post like this one, which is covered in strong rope.

Cat litter box

Litter boxes are indoor toilets for cats and are available in various styles. Those with hoods are probably the best. They give your pet some privacy and the litter won't get scattered around the sides. You will need to fill the box with cat litter. Soiled cat litter can be removed with a scoop.

● *Above: A litter box is an essential item for a cat. The type that has a plastic hood is very useful because it will stop loose cat litter from being scattered outside the box.*

The cat flap

If one of your doors is fitted with a cat flap, your cat will be able to come and go as it pleases. There are several types of cat flap available, including some that will open only for your pet if it wears a special collar. Make sure that the flap is neither too high nor too low for your cat.

22

Keeping your pet safe

All cats and kittens are inquisitive so it is important to make your home and garden "cat safe!" This is similar to making it safe for a young child.

Safety in the home

Make sure that your cat can't come into contact with household cleaning fluids, such as bleach. Electric cords can be a danger to a playful kitten. A frayed cord could easily electrocute your pet. Always keep sharp things, such as knives and pins out of the reach of your pet. Keep the washing machine, wardrobe doors, and cupboard drawers shut, so that your pet doesn't get trapped inside.

Road safety

Inquisitive kittens may get onto busy roads through open doors, so it is important to close the front and back doors carefully. Make sure that all upper floor windows are secure, especially in hot weather, as a kitten could easily climb out and have a nasty fall.

Safety in the garden

Some plants, such as Rhododendron, Azalea, Sweet Pea, and Clematis are poisonous to cats. It is best not to have too many in your garden and you should make sure that your cat can't come into contact with them. Poisonous liquids such as pesticides, together with sharp gardening equipment like shears and rakes, should always be safely locked away.

Garden ponds

These should not have steep sides so that your cat can climb out easily if it falls in. It would be safer to have a net stretched over the water to stop your cat or kitten falling in. This will also help to prevent your cat pestering any fish or pond life that are in your pond!

Hygiene

Cats are very clean creatures. They always dig a hole
before going to the toilet and cover it up afterward.
They also groom themselves every day. They are
likely to turn their noses up at dirty food dishes or
litter boxes that aren't spotlessly clean.

Feeding bowls

To keep your pet in good health it is essential to
keep all its equipment clean. Feeding bowls should
be washed thoroughly every day and scraps of old
food removed. This is especially important in hot
weather. You should never wash your pet's dishes
with your own because you could spread germs.

Litter box

Soiled litter should be removed from your cat's litter
box with a scoop. At least once a week, the litter box
should be emptied and scrubbed clean. You can get
safe disinfectant from your pet supply store or your
vet. You should always wash your hands after
cleaning your pet's litter box.

● *Above: You don't need to change all your cat's litter
every day as long as you remove soiled litter frequently.*

The bed

Your cat's bedding should be washed every month to keep it fresh. Even the cleanest cats can have fleas and their eggs can drop off into their bedding and cause an infestation. If this happens, ask your pet supply store or vet for a spray or powder that will kill both flea eggs and larvae and treat your pet and its bedding. Because all cats can get fleas from time to time, you should not let your pet sleep on your own bed.

Brushes and combs

Grooming equipment, such as combs and brushes, should be washed after use and thoroughly cleaned once a month.

● *Right: Grooming your cat regularly with a special comb will help to remove dead hairs from its coat.*

CHECKLIST – Hygiene

● Keep your cat's food bowls scrupulously clean.

● Remove soiled litter from the litter box every day.

● Always wash your hands thoroughly after emptying the litter box.

Feeding your cat

A proper diet is important to keep your cat or kitten
healthy. Young, active cats need a lot of protein and
fat in their diet. You can feed them prepared or fresh
food, or a mixture of both. Prepared foods have the
advantage over fresh foods because they contain all
the nutritional requirements your cat needs.

Types of prepared food

There are three types of prepared foods: dried,
semimoist, and canned. Dried food comes in the
form of biscuits and is useful because it will keep for
a long time once it is in the feeding bowl. You must
make sure that your cat has lots of drinking water if
you feed it dried food. Semimoist food contains
water and comes in the form of soft morsels.

● **Above:** *Prepared foods are a convenient way of giving
your cat a balanced diet. Lots of clean, fresh water (1) is
essential if your cat eats dried food (2). Canned food (3)
comes in many different flavors. Store it in the fridge after
opening to keep it fresh. Semimoist food (4) comes in the
form of soft morsels.*

Using canned food

If you don't use a whole can of food you will have to
store the remaining portion in the fridge. You will
need to let the food reach room temperature again
before serving it to your cat. You can get canned
"kitten" food for growing kittens, which contains all
the essential vitamins and minerals they require.

How much to give

When giving prepared foods, follow the feeding
instructions carefully. Kittens need a small meal four
or five times a day until they are about six months
old. Over the next six months, feeding can gradually
be reduced to twice a day. Adult cats should be fed
twice a day. Some cats will eat all their food at once,
while others prefer to nibble throughout the day.

● *Above: Cats are very particular and will usually only
eat their food if it is served at room temperature.*

Drinks

Some cats and kittens have problems digesting milk and it upsets their stomachs. You can buy milk mixtures especially made for cats which don't cause this problem. It is essential that your cat or kitten always has fresh, clean drinking water. Your cat may not seem to drink much water when you are feeding it canned food. This is because there is water in the food. Even so, it is still important to give your cat fresh water every day. Your pet will require a small, shallow food dish together with a small water bowl.

Fresh food

If you give your cat fresh food it is best to give it prepared food as well to make sure that it gets all the right vitamins and minerals. All meat should be thoroughly cooked, any bones removed, and the meat chopped into small pieces. Canned sardines or tuna make a nutritious meal. Boiled or steamed fish can also be served, but make sure you remove all the bones first.

Varying the diet

It is a good idea to vary your cat's diet as much as possible. This will prevent it becoming a fussy eater and will give your pet a balanced and interesting diet.

Eating grass

Cats instinctively eat grass and this often makes them throw up. However this can be a good thing because the cat will bring up any fur it has swallowed at the same time. Fur that the cat has swallowed while grooming itself can clump together in its stomach as "fur balls" and make it ill.

● **Below:** *It is natural behavior for cats to eat grass. It is a good idea to give a cat that is kept indoors a regular supply. You can do this by growing some in a tray.*

Questions *and* Answers

When can I feed cat treats to my pet?
Treats can be fed in small quantities during the day. They can make a delicious reward for your cat when you are training it.

Do cats need milk to drink?
Cats do not usually need cow's milk to drink. It can upset their stomachs and give them diarrhea. You can get special milk that won't make your cat sick from pet supply stores and it might prefer this instead.

My cat does not seem to drink very much. Is this normal?
If you are feeding your cat canned food, most of the water the cat requires is contained within the food. However, fresh, clean water should be available to your cat at all times especially if it is fed wholly on dried food.

Will my cat eat too much?
Usually cats do not overeat. But there is always one greedy pet! It is not healthy for your cat to become fat, so don't be tempted to feed it between meals and check its weight regularly.

My cat won't eat its food when it comes right out of the fridge. Why is this?
Cats can be very fussy eaters and usually don't like chilled food. If you have to store part of a can of cat food in the fridge your cat may refuse to eat it. If this is the case put the food in your pet's bowl and let it return to room temperature before you serve it.

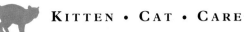

● *Above:* Prepared foods such as canned food, dried food, and semimoist food are very convenient and will provide a good diet. You can introduce variety into your cat's diet by giving it fresh, cooked meat and fish on a regular basis.

● *Above:* Although lots of cats like milk, some cannot digest it and it upsets their stomachs. You could offer them easily-digestible cat milk or water instead.

31

Grooming and handling

You should regularly brush and comb your cat to keep its coat in good condition. Short-haired cats need grooming once or twice a week. Long-haired cats need grooming at least three times a week.

Grooming the coat
Gently brush through your cat's fur from head to tail. Don't forget to comb your cat's underside. Check the comb for small black specks. These could be a sign of fleas.

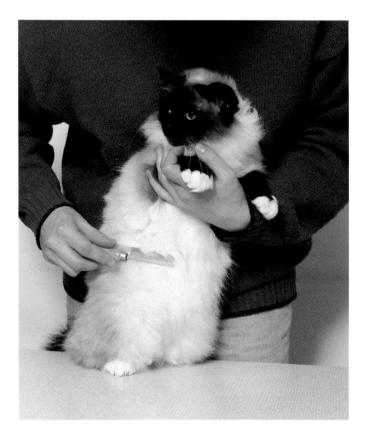

● *Above: A good time to check your cat's coat for fleas is during grooming. Use a fine-tooth comb and examine the coat and dead hair for black specks.*

● **Above:** *You should regularly clean the inside of your cat's ears with wipes to prevent infections.*

Eyes, ears, and teeth

Gently clean around the eyes using a separate wipe for each eye. Gently clean inside your cat's ears as well. Never poke anything into the ear. This may damage the middle and inner ear. Cotton batting should be avoided because stray fibers can cause eye and ear infections. Check teeth regularly to make sure that they are clean.

Claws

Long claws can give a nasty scratch and cause pad infections. If your cat's claws need trimming ask an adult to help you. Your vet will tell you which type of claw clippers are the most suitable for your pet.

Trimming the claws

Position your cat in front of you with its back toward you. Hold a paw gently but firmly in one hand and press it lightly to extend the claws. Cut off the white part of the claw. This will not hurt your pet. Do not cut the claw where it is pink and sensitive.

● **Above:** *It is important to get used to handling your cat properly. If you lift your pet awkwardly you could hurt it.*

Bathing your pet

You won't usually need to bath your cat. However, you must if it gets anything dirty on its fur. Lower your cat into a bath of warm water filled about 6 in (15 cm) deep. Wet its coat thoroughly and massage in cat shampoo. Be careful not to get any soap into your pet's eyes. Rinse its fur thoroughly. Lift your cat out of the water and wrap it in a towel. Short-haired cats can be left to dry naturally in a warm house. Long-haired cats may be dried with a blow dryer on a low setting. Comb the cat's fur when it is dry.

Handling

It is much easier to learn how to handle your cat correctly when it is a small, light kitten. To pick your kitten up, place one hand under its body behind its front legs and gently lift it. Using your other hand, scoop up the rear of your kitten. Then hold its front legs securely with one hand and its hind legs with your other. Support the weight of your kitten using your forearm. In this position, your kitten should be quite comfortable. When your kitten grows up you should still be able to hold it in this position.

CHECKLIST – Grooming

- Always ask an adult to help you to trim your cat's claws.

- Check your cat's fur regularly for fleas. This is best done during grooming.

- Long-haired cats will need frequent grooming to prevent their fur from getting matted.

35

Training your cat

Training
Cats can't be trained in the same way as dogs but you can make your pet "house-friendly" with a little coaxing. Never smack or hit your cat or kitten. If your pet does something which is not allowed, say "No!" sharply. If this fails, clap your hands loudly.

● *Above: A cat flap will let your cat go in and out as it pleases. Some can be locked if you want to keep your pet in.*

Scratching post
If there is one particular piece of furniture that your cat likes to scratch, place the scratching post in front of it. If you see your pet scratching the furniture, shout "No!" and then gently place its front paws on the scratching post.

The litter box
For the first few days after bringing your kitten home, place it regularly in its litter box and it should soon get the right idea. Leave the box where your kitten can easily get to it and always keep it in the same place, well away from its food and water bowl.

Cat flap
Cats are quick to understand how to use cat flaps. If you push them gently through a few times and reward them on the other side with a few cat treats they'll soon learn.

Lead walking

Some cats, especially Siamese, will walk on a lead. A cat that regularly walks on a lead will need to wear a harness. Put the harness on your cat for short periods of time. When it is used to this, attach the lead. Don't try to "walk" your cat at this stage. After a while, try walking your cat around your backyard. With time and patience you should be successful.

Collars

You should get your new kitten used to wearing a collar with a name and address tag attached to it. Then, if your pet goes missing, it can be identified and returned to you. You should only buy collars that are specially designed for cats. These have extra elastic and will stretch enough for your cat to get its head out if the collar gets caught on a twig.

● **Above:** *Some cats enjoy walking on a lead. If you walk your cat regularly it should wear a special harness.*

Providing exercise and toys

All cats need exercise. If your cat is allowed outdoors it will probably get enough exercise to keep it fit and healthy. Cats which are kept indoors can become lazy and bored and it might be best to have two cats so they can give each other essential animal contact and play. Cats that are kept indoors will benefit from a scratching post. A wooden platform allows your cat to climb and sit in a high place as it would outdoors.

Playing with toys

Cats enjoy playing. You can buy all sorts of toys in pet supply stores, but often a large cardboard box will be appreciated just as much. Small balls, with or without bells, are another favorite toy. Cats love to play with anything bobbing around on the end of a piece of string. However, don't leave your pet on its own to play with this kind of toy. It has been known for cats to get tangled up in a long piece of string and choke themselves.

● **Above:** *Cats love to play and will chase anything that moves!*

An outdoor run

If your cat has an outdoor run it should be as large
as possible and fitted with shelves of varying heights.
You can also put a tree stump or scratching post in
the run. A waterproof shelter should be provided.

During the day

Many cats sleep for long periods in the daytime.
Leaving your cat alone in the house during the day
should not create any major problems as long as it
has enough food, water, a litter box, and toys.

● *Above:* If your cat can't
roam free and has an outdoor
run, you could add a length of
tree trunk to make your pet's
environment more interesting.

39

Breeding cats and caring for the kittens

Breeding cats
You should not allow your cat to breed unless you can care for the mother and homes can be found for the kittens. Ask your vet about neutering, which will prevent unwanted pregnancies.

When cats can have kittens
Female cats (queens) can have their first litter of kittens when they are about 7 to 12 months old. Male cats (toms) can father kittens when they are between 10 and 15 months old. Queens can only become pregnant at certain times and this is known as coming into season. The queen can come into season every two weeks at certain times of the year. The season lasts for two to four days.

Signs of pregnancy
Signs of pregnancy can usually be seen after about

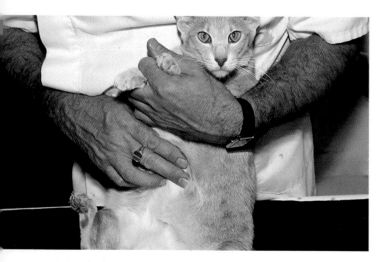

three weeks. A pregnant cat will have reddened teats and a swollen abdomen and will gradually gain weight. The pregnancy lasts for approximately 65

days. A pregnant cat does not require extra attention other than being fed a well-balanced and nourishing diet. Vets sometimes prescribe extra vitamins and minerals at this time.

● **Above:** *A pregnant queen with well-rounded tummy. Your vet will be able to detect signs of pregnancy in your pet after about three weeks. (Left)*

Preparing for the birth

A pregnant cat can be allowed outside until two weeks before the kittens are due to be born. She must then be kept indoors. You should prepare a box for your cat where she can be warm and comfortable and where she can give birth without being disturbed. Line the box with newspaper.

The birth

Cats usually give birth without difficulty or human help, but let your vet know as soon as your cat goes into labor so that you can get help if there are any problems. When labor begins, the queen will start to pant heavily. This first stage can last up to six hours.

BREEDING CATS AND CARING FOR THE KITTENS

The second stage is when the queen pushes out a kitten. If there is no kitten after she has pushed for 30 minutes you should contact your vet. The third stage is when the placenta is delivered. The queen licks each kitten clean. She also instinctively bites through the umbilical cords. The size of the litter is usually between two and six kittens and a kitten will be born about every half an hour.

After the birth

When the birth is over, the mother should be provided with water, food, and a litter box. The bedding in the box where the kittens were born should be changed. The mother will require lots of highly nutritious food while she feeds her kittens. For the first few days it is better not to disturb the cat and her kittens very much. It is important to keep the kittens warm when they are really young.

Feeding the kittens

After the birth, the mother produces milk for her kittens and they will usually start to feed from her within two hours of being born.

Gradually, the kittens stop relying on their mother for milk and will be ready to start eating solid food. This is known as weaning.

Weaning the kittens

You can begin weaning the kittens when they are about three weeks old. Gradually introduce them to simple foods, such as dried cat food soaked in milk and by 10 weeks old they should be fully weaned and eating solid food. Kittens can be separated from their mother and taken to a new home at about 10 weeks of age but don't separate them before this time. They rely on their mother to teach them important skills.

● *Left: A proud mother nurses her kittens. The kittens are dependent on their mother for the first 10 weeks of life and she produces milk to feed them. Make sure she has a really good diet while she is feeding them.*

Cat behavior

Different moods

The happy cat walks confidently with its tail held high. Its fur is smooth and it looks relaxed. An aggressive cat will have its ears pricked backward and its claws and teeth showing. The pupils of its eyes will be closed to slits while its whiskers will bristle forward. Its bushed-up tail will be twitching and held low. A defensive cat standing its ground will arch its body and its fur will bristle along the length of its back. The tail will be arched and bushy. The cat's ears will be flattened and the whiskers bristling. The pupils will be large and the mouth will be open, baring the cat's teeth.

● *Above: It is obvious from this cat's flattened ears and bared teeth that it is angry about something. Cats are very good at communicating their feelings and use lots of different signals to show what kind of mood they are in.*

Communication

Sounds are an important form of communication for all animals. A cat can make many sounds, from quiet purring to noisy yowling. Purring usually means that your cat is contented. Cats can also purr when they are frightened or in pain. Some cats "talk" more than others, especially the Oriental breeds such as the Siamese. This is because some cats tend to be more dominant than others.

Marking territory

A cat's sense of smell is well developed and it uses it to recognise its territory. When you return home your cat will often rub against your legs several times before going away to lick itself. This is a cat's way of accepting and claiming ownership of you by marking you with its scent.

● **Above:** *The Siamese is one of the noisiest and liveliest breeds of cat. Siamese cats are really vocal and some will "talk" all day! They are very good at letting their owners know exactly how they feel and demand lots of attention.*

Mixing with other pets

Usually kittens are not fully weaned off their mother's milk before they are eight weeks old. Normally, you can introduce a new kitten to your home when it is about 10 weeks old. If you already have other pets it is best to introduce your kitten to them when it is slightly older, at 12-14 weeks.

Introducing your new pet

Introducing your new kitten to your other animals requires patience. It is a good idea to keep your new kitten in a secure pen for the first few days. This will allow it to become used to its surroundings, and also let your other pets get to know it. It is important that you give your other pets attention. They could easily become jealous.

Meeting existing pets

If you have more than one pet, introduce the new kitten to each animal individually. Other cats may hiss and even attack a new kitten. Although you must prevent the kitten from being harmed, try not to interfere. A dog must be kept under firm control when introducing it to the new kitten. Do not allow the dog to get too close to the kitten until you are sure that they have become used to one another. Usually, it takes two to four weeks for other pets to accept a new kitten as a member of the household.

● *Left:* As this picture shows, cats and dogs can sometimes be the best of friends! If you are patient when you introduce a new kitten or cat to existing pets they will probably tolerate each other. Take care not to make your pets jealous of the newcomer, though.

Going on vacation

Using a cattery

Your cat or kitten cannot be left unsupervised while you are away on vacation, so you will have to make arrangements for its care. One solution is to board your pet in a cattery. You will have to book it a place well before your vacation especially during the

summer months. If you want to leave your cat or
kitten in a cattery you will have to make sure that it
has had all the necessary vaccinations. All good
catteries will want to see an up-to-date vaccination
certificate. Your vet will be able to tell you what you
need to do and may be able to recommend a cattery.

Inspecting catteries

Inspect the cattery first
before you decide to
book your pet in, to
make sure it is clean and
secure and that the cats
already there are happy
and healthy. Ask the
cattery owners what you
will need to bring with
your pet for its stay.

Using a pet sitter

If you have a friend or
neighbor who can
guarantee to visit your
home every day to check
on your cat and feed it,
then you could leave
your pet in your home.
Your friend will also
have to clean out the
cat's litter box every
day, so make sure they
know what is involved
before they agree!

● **Left:** *Cats being
boarded in a cattery. You
must make proper care
arrangements for your pet
before you go away.*

Keeping your cat healthy

Prolonged sleeping, lack of interest in food, or hiding can be the signs of an unhealthy cat. Feeding changes such as loss of appetite or excessive drinking could also indicate a health problem.

Symptoms to watch for

If your cat has difficulty walking or is in pain, it is possible that it has been involved in a traffic accident

and may be bleeding internally. Frequent vomiting, diarrhea and/or passing blood when it uses its litter

box are also causes for concern. Your cat can quickly become dehydrated and if these symptoms continue it is essential that you contact your vet as quickly as possible. Frequent sneezing and/or coughing, or difficulty in breathing are signs that your pet may have a respiratory problem. Contact your vet for advice if you notice any of these symptoms.

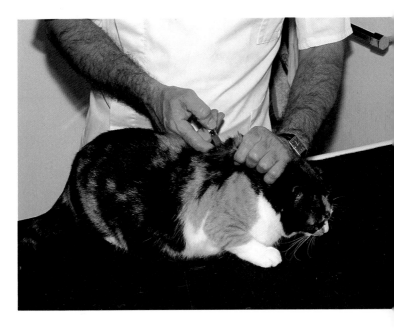

Vaccinations
It is important to protect your cat from infectious diseases by having it regularly vaccinated. Two of the most common cat diseases are Feline enteritis and cat flu. Your vet will be able to start a course of vaccinations against these illnesses when your kitten is about 12 weeks old. Once a year, your pet will need "booster" injections to reinforce the vaccinations.

● **Above:** *You should take your cat to the vet every year to be vaccinated. Your vet will be able to offer advice if your cat seems to be ill. (Left)*

51

Eyes

If your cat's eyes run constantly this could be a sign that your pet has an eye infection. Your vet will be able to supply you with drops to treat this problem.

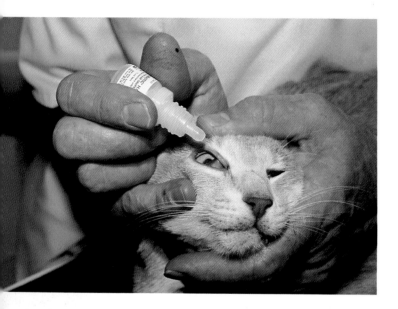

Ears

Inflammation or constant scratching of the ears could mean that your cat has an ear infection, so ask your vet for advice.

Teeth

If your cat's gums are red and it has dirty teeth or bad breath it may have a gum disease called gingivitis. This is common in cats and is caused by a build up of tartar on the teeth. Your vet will be able to clean your cat's teeth.

● *Above:* *A cat with an eye infection having eye drops applied by a vet. Ask your vet to show you how to give the drops properly. You will probably have to continue the treatment at home until your cat is better.*

Fleas

Excessive scratching or frantic licking could be a sign that your pet has fleas. Check your cat's coat for flea droppings regularly. These look like fine black specks. If you find evidence of fleas, see your vet or pet supply store as soon as possible for advice on treatment. It is important to kill both the flea eggs and larvae, so ask for a product that will do both and treat your cat and its bedding. Your cat should wear a flea collar to help prevent fleas.

Worms

Weight loss or diarrhea could mean your cat has internal worms. Your vet will be able to supply you with suitable worming medicine. To prevent worms give your cat a worm tablet regularly; every four months to prevent tapeworms and every six months to prevent roundworms.

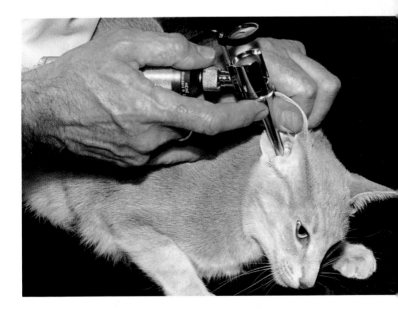

● ***Above:*** *A vet looks inside a cat's ears during an examination using an instrument called an auroscope.*

Visiting the vet

Registering your new pet

It is a good idea to take your cat or kitten to the vet
for regular check-ups and vaccinations. When you
bring your new pet home, it is wise to register it with
a veterinary clinic. Take your new cat or kitten to the
vet as soon as possible for a check-up and to discuss
its health requirements. There may be times when
your cat could become ill and it will help if the clinic
is familiar with your pet.

Choosing a pet carrier

Whether you are bringing your cat or kitten home for
the first time, or transporting it to the vet or to a
cattery you will need to keep your pet secure. There
are many kinds of pet carriers available, either made
of cardboard, suitable for emergencies, or plastic or
wicker, suitable for regular use.

Transporting your pet

When you are transporting your cat or kitten, place a
clean towel or newspaper in the bottom of the
carrier. Pick your cat up gently but firmly, put it into
the carrier, close the door quickly and fasten it
securely. Do not leave your cat unattended when it is
inside the carrier. When transporting your pet take
care not to let it become overheated or too cold.

At the vet's clinic

When you arrive at the vet's clinic confirm your
appointment with the receptionist. Keep your cat's
carrier close to you. Don't be tempted to open it or
to let your cat out. When your turn comes, introduce
your pet to the vet and explain what the problem is.
It will help the vet if you can describe all the changes
that you have noticed in your cat's behavior.

● *Right: Take your cat to the vet in a safe, secure carrier
and make sure that it can't get out.*

In an emergency

Moving the cat to safety
If your cat is involved in a traffic accident you will
need to act quickly. Remove your cat from danger by
gently placing a sheet underneath it and lifting it to a
safe place. Contact your vet immediately. While you
are waiting for the vet to arrive there are some things
you can do to help your cat.

First aid
Check that your cat has a pulse.
You can find it on the inside of the cat's thigh where
it joins the body.

Check your cat's breathing by placing your hand on
its chest. If it is irregular or non-existent, open the
cat's mouth, pull the tongue forward and check that
the airway is clear.

Check the heartbeat. This can be felt on the chest
behind the front legs.

Heavy bleeding can be stopped by pressing the wound with a clean cloth pad.

Your cat may go into shock. Keep it warm with blankets.

If you think that your cat has broken bones, do not try to move it unless you absolutely have to. If you do have to move it because of traffic or other dangers carefully slide your pet onto a flat board first.

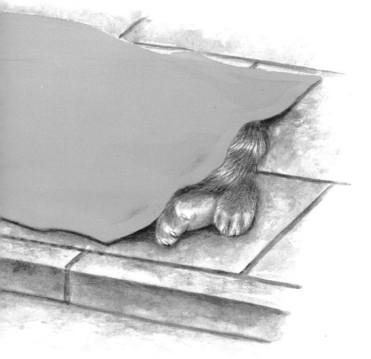

● *Above: An injured cat may go into shock, so keep it warm with blankets while you wait for help to arrive.*

Emergency first aid kit

This should contain safe disinfectant, eye wash, antiseptic cream, adhesive dressing, and cotton batting.

Questions *and* Answers

How long does a cat live?
A healthy, well cared for cat that is regularly seen by a vet and vaccinated against the most common infectious cat diseases can live for 15 years and may even survive into its twenties.

What is the best way to give medicine to my cat?
The easiest way to give a tablet to your cat is to crush it into a fine powder and mix it into the cat's food. However, some cats can sense the tablet and will refuse to eat their food. If this is the case, ask an adult to help you to open your cat's mouth by pressing gently at each side of its jaws. You can then drop the tablet far back onto the tongue. Wait a few seconds to make sure your cat doesn't spit the tablet out again.

How should I care for my sick cat?
If your cat is ill, it must be kept warm, quiet, and safe. Provide it with a comfortable resting place and a well-balanced diet recommended by your vet. Your cat must not go outside until you are absolutely certain that it has recovered.

How can I keep my cat healthy?
There are four ways to try to keep your cat in good health. Many cats die in traffic accidents so try to make sure that your cat cannot get onto busy roads. Keep your cat's feeding bowls and bedding clean. Take your cat to the vet for regular check-ups. Make sure your cat is up to date with all its vaccinations.

● *Above:* A contented, well cared for cat sitting in the sun. With proper care, your cat may live for many years.

59

CARE CHECKLIST

DAILY CHECKLIST

- Wash all feeding utensils.
- Supply fresh drinking water.

Feeding
- Kittens require food up to five times a day.
- Adult cats require food twice a day.

- Handling.
- Play.
- Remove soiled litter.

WEEKLY CHECKLIST

Grooming
- Short-haired - twice a week.
- Long-haired - at least three times a week.
- Check and trim claws if necessary (with adult help).
- Check for fleas.

Feeding
- Vary the diet.
- Wash out litter box.

MONTHLY CHECKLIST

- Wash bedding and grooming equipment.

About my cat

MY CAT'S NAME IS
_____

_____

MY CAT'S BIRTHDAY IS
_____

Stick a photo of your pet here

WHICH BREED? MY CAT IS A
_____

_____

MY CAT'S FAVORITE FOOD IS
_____

_____

MY CAT'S FAVORITE TOY IS
_____

_____

MY VET'S NAME IS
_____

_____

MY VET'S TELEPHONE NUMBER IS
_____

_____

Index